DDR!

Mini Book Series

VOLUME XXV

By

Ronald Pattinson

1st edition

Published in August 2016 by

Kilderkin
171 hs Warmondstraat, Amsterdam, Noord- Holland

ISBN 978-94-90270-29-2

Contents

Foreword

The DDR and me. It was and still is a complex relationship.

Scummy Brit that I am, I loved the low, low prices and . . . I was thinking of something else to praise, but it really was the prices that got me. That and some of the most engaged and fun people I'd ever met.

I still can't quite explain my relationship with the DDR to myself. Let alone anyone else. I still dream of shopping in a HO supermarket with Ostmarks. It's an optimistic dream. My ten marks get me a half bottle of Korn and a bagfull of Eisenacher Helles.

I could pretend this is a considered appreciation of my time in the less-fashionable German state. It isn't. Just a load of random crap about the first workers' and peasants' state on German soil.

Ron Pattinson.

Amsterdam, 9th August 2016.

Explanation

The final days of the DDR were a special time for me. Not always special in the right way, but magical nonetheless. Jumping through bureaucratic hoops and finally marrying Dolores. Then moving to Swindon.

In the run up to our marriage in 1988, I spent a lot of time in the DDR. And came to love it. As anyone would. Beer was under a quid a pint and don't get me started about spirits.

So many happy days in Berlin. With Cabaret and Funeral in Berlin always in the back of my mind. A wonderful, magical city, with U-bahn's from the West rattling under Friedrichstrasse through bricked-up stations, and West Berlin shining provocatively at the end of the street.

It's a lost world. Disappeared, never to return, like the Hapsburgs and the Hohenzollerns.

Think Swindon's still there, mind.

I Looking back

The good old days

Since 1989 much has been said about the poor quality of DDR beer, mostly by those who never drank a drop of it themselves. Much is made of the lack of adherence to the Reinheitsgebot and the lack of investment.

To begin with the former, pils and special beers were usually brewed with around 85% malt - a percentage perfectly acceptable in most countries. In any case, how well-established is the Reinheitsgebot in the former Prussian territories. As far as I am aware, it only came into force in the whole of Germany after 1906, previously having been a purely Bavarian law. Given that it was ignored during the two world wars, this means it was only in force in E. Berlin 1906 - 1914 and 1919 - 1939. An impressive 28 out of the 750 years the city has been around.

As for the lack of investment and old-fashioned equipment; the same commentators who denounce this in the DDR, are charmed by it elsewhere. Look at the praise heaped on Cantillon or Oud Beersel in Belgium for being museums.

East Berlin Beer

On the more subjective matter of taste, the Berliner Weisse brewed by the VEB Schultheiss Brauerei Schönhauser Allee (Abt. Weissbier) was the classic version of the beer, unfiltered, unpasteurised, uncompromising in its flavour, and definitely far superior to its western counterpart. The closure, in the 1990's, of the brewery which produced it was a tragedy for beer lovers. It had also been the first home of the revived Leipziger Gose, when the style was brewed again in the mid-80's after a 20-year break.

Amongst pils beers, the old Bärenquell Berliner Spezial was probably the best of all Berlin, more assertive and characterful than its western counterparts. When served on draught, not only were the eastern beers a good deal cheaper (around 1M for a 0.5 litre) but were much less likely to be ruined by excessive top pressure or chilling.

Not that everything was perfect. To carry out a pub crawl required an encyclopaedic knowledge of the diverse and bizarre opening times and a good deal of luck when trying to find a seat. Often pubs were unspecific about which brewery was supplying the beer and the choice available was fairly limited. With the exception of a couple of places selling Czech beer or posh hotels with Radeberger, there was only really locally-produced stuff available. But what's so wrong with that, when the area has a decent number of proficient brewers? (Go to Munich and try looking for beer from outside the city.)

A tragic (but thankfully, temporary) loss was the Weissbierstube, which was in one of the shopping arcades by the Rotes Rathaus. They sold a whole range of cocktails made with (the real) Berliner Weisse. (If you look below, you'll be pleased to read that it's open again).

Berlin is home to an annual beer festival, claimed to be the largest event of its kind in Germany. Started in 1997, it takes place in the open air, along the Karl-Marx-Allee between the Frankfurter Tor and Strausberger Platz (the last time I was out that way was to pick up some documents for my wedding from the DDR Innenministerium).

If you want to get an idea of what drinking was like in East Berlin before the wall was breached, take a glance at an article I wrote in 1989: "Get Weisse behind the wall: A guide to pubs in East Berlin".

To be more positive, beers from old DDR breweries have made a strong comeback in the eastern parts of Berlin. The consumer's choice has been greatly augmented by the introduction of Czech dark lagers on draught. In Prenzlauer Berg, always a good spot for a pub crawl and a re-enactment of selected scenes from Cabaret, new 'Szenekneipen', trendy bars, have sprung up in recent years.

Now, if I could only find a drop of the old Mühlhausener Pilsator on draught somewhere.

II Get Weisse behind the wall

Introduction

EAST BERLIN, over-shadowed by its western half, is nevertheless a city of considerable architectural interest.

Not least of those attractions are the old pubs and many of them have managed to survive both the bombs of the RAF and post-war reconstruction.

To discover the unspoilt gems, you have to stray away from the usual tourist path of Unter den Linden, Alexanderplatz, and Friedrichstrasse and make an excursion to Prenzlauer Berg.

Lying a mile or so north of Alexanderplatz, this old working-class district is the largest surviving area of pre-war buildings anywhere in Berlin, East or West. Full of turn-of-the-century tenement blocks, many rather in need of repair, it conjures up the atmosphere of the Berlin of the Weimar republic.

Schönhauser Alle, one of its main thoroughfares, contains a string of night clubs and late bars, but most of the entertainment is provided by small, local pubs hidden among the back streets.

Beers

East Berlin has several breweries, whose beers are sold under a variety of names including Kindl and Schultheiss, which are also used by different, private breweries in

West Berlin. The signs outside pubs do not really indicate what is on sale inside - for instance, there are signs still for Burgerbräu, a brew which no longer exists [This statement is totally untrue - not only was Burgerbräu still brewing in 1989, it's one of the few remaining large breweries in Berlin today. R.P.] - or many simply say "Berliner Bier".

All of this can make it difficult to know exactly which brewery the beer came from. The beer types are:

Weisse: a top-fermented beer made with a mixture of wheat and barley malt of around 9° Balling. It is naturally conditioned when bottled and on draught unfiltered and full of sediment. It is usually drunk mixed with a sweet, red fruit syrup or" Schuss". To get just the beer it should be ordered "ohne Schuss".

Hell: a cheap pale lager, often rather thin. It isn't usually sold on draught in Berlin, but can be found in bottles in supermarkets.

Pils: The standard beer, a pale lager of around 11.5° Balling. It is often unpasteurised even in bottled form, and the better examples are pleasantly bitter and drinkable.

Pilsator: A premium version of Pils of around 12.5° Balling. It is higher quality and fuller-bodied, but unfortunately usually pasteurised in its bottled form. A common bottled version is Echt Berliner.

Bock: A strong bottled winter beer of around 16° Balling, which comes in both pale and dark versions.

Porter: A top-fermented bottled porter of around 18° Balling can occasionally be found in shops.

Pubs

Apart from when you sit at the bar, waiter service is the norm in the DDR. Standing is not usually permitted, which means if you want a drink you have to find a seat.

This is not always as easy as it sounds. "Reserved" signs often adorn tables that are obviously going to remain unused all day. DDR waiters also have a great sense of order and hence a pathological hatred of the furniture being rearranged.

Any attempt to move a chair from one table to another is usually met with a strict reprimand. All this means that it is unwise to attempt a pub crawl.

Though most bars are run by HO, a state company that covers all types of retail outlets such as shops and restaurants, there are also some private pubs.

Pub Listings

Assuming that most people enter East Berlin by Checkpoint Charlie or the Friedrichstrasse S and U-Bahn station, the most logical place to begin is Friedrichstrasse itself. In the ground floor of the new Grand Hotel on the corner of Unter den Linden is **Stammhaus Kindl** (open 10-24), a specialist beer bar.

It serves a wide range of beers from the DDR, plus a couple from Czechoslovakia. The selection includes Berliner Pilsator and Weisse, Wernesgrüner Pils, Radeburger Pils, Pilsener Urquell and Budvar.

The interior is plush, all leather, mahogany and brass. It's obvious that a lot of money was spent on the décor and this is reflected in the prices, which are the most expensive in the DDR at around 6M for half a litre.

Not the place for meeting the locals for only West German tourists can afford to drink here, but worth a visit to sample a slightly wider range of beer.

Walking down Unter den Linden away from the Brandenburg Gate, past the Dom and across the River Spree by the Palast Hotel you come to Spandauer Strasse. Take a right turn and you will come to the Marx-Engels-Forum, a parade of fashionable shops by the Rotes Rathaus.

Here is the **Weissbierstube** (10-24) a small, new pub specialising in Berliner Weisse. It sells Berliner Pilsator and Weisse, and offers various Weisse cocktails. Its two small rooms are simply furnished and feature some attractive, if rather enigmatic, enamel signs.

Between Spandauer Strasse and the River Spree is the Nikolai Viertiel, a newly-renovated area around the restored Nikolai Kirche. The idea was to recreate some of the old core of the city and, with its mixture of reconstruction and new buildings designed to blend in, it works reasonably well.

On Am Nussbaum is one of the reconstructions, **Zum Nussbaum** (10-24), which sells Berliner Pilsator, Weisse and Echt Berliner. The original, which included the artist Zille among its regulars, was built in 1571 but destroyed by bombing in 1943. The new version has a cosy and reasonably authentic atmosphere, with several small, rather cramped rooms. It also sells good, if rather expensive for the DDR, snacks.

It is only a short walk to Alexanderplatz from where you can take the U-Bahn to Prenzlauer Berg. Take the line in the direction Pankow (Vinetastrasse) and get off at Senefelderpiatz. This will bring you to within a hundred metres of the next stopping off point, the **Metzer Eck** (16-1) on the corner of Metzerstrasse and Strassbourgerstrasse.

The street has the crumbling plaster facades typical of the whole area, but don't be put off by the apparent dilapidation, for this is the real Berlin. The Metzer Eck is a small private pub, with a few more personal decorative touches than the standard HO bars, but with the same low prices. Here half a litre of Berliner Pils should cost you just over 1M.

Walking back along Metzerstrasse and then turning right up Kollwitzerstrasse you will come to Kollwitplatz. On the opposite side of this pleasant little square is Husemannstrasse, a street which has been restored to its original turn-of-the-century appearance. It features a whole array of old shops - a chemist, a greengrocer and, of course a pub, **Budike 15** (10-22) [Husemanstrasse 15]. It sells Berliner Pilsator, Weisse and Echt Berliner and has simple wooden furniture.

Continuing along Husemannstrasse, you come to Dimitroffstrasse [today Danzigerstrasse R.P]. Turn left and you will come to **Zum Hackepeter** (Wed-Thu 15-24, Fri-Sun 15-1, Mon-Tue closed). This basic corner local sells Berliner Pilsator and Weisse, During the 20's this was a Nazi "Stammlokal" while the pub opposite, **Zum Schusterjungen** [Danziger Str. 9,10435 Berlin] (11-23), was used by the communists. It is an unpretentious two-room affair offering Berliner Pils and Weisse and reasonable cheap food.

Just before the junction of Dimitroffstrasse and Schönhauser Allee is Pappelallee, another street that has seen better days. About 100 metres along on the left is **Kohlensaure Niederlage** (Wed-Fri 11-21, Sat-Sun 10-21, Mon-Tue closed), which may be a little difficult to spot because of its almost illegible sign. Inside is a genuine untouched old Berlin local selling Berliner Pils, and boasting an antique fruit machine among its sparse furnishings. The atmosphere, like the décor, is down-to-earth and friendly.

A little further up Pappelallee, on the opposite side of the street is **Zur Pappel** (Mon-Thu 11-21, Fri-Sun 14-24) serving Berliner Pils. This one-room pub has an impressive old wooden bar and a bizarre balcony at the rear. The standard 1960's HO tubular steel tables may detract a little from the charm, but it's still a pleasant enough place in which to drink a pint or two.

Continuing along Pappelallee, over the S-Bahn line, where it becomes Stahlheimerstraße, you will eventually come to **Humannklause** on the left-hand side of the street. It sells Berliner Weisse and Pils (outside are some rather nice Schultheiss signs, but who knows if that is really the source of the beer). Inside, it's more comfortable than most of the other pubs in the area.

On the last side street before the end of Stahlheimerstrasse, is **Bräustübl** (Mon-Fri 16-24, Sat 9-13, Sun closed) which offers Berliner Pils. Housed in the ground floor of a 1920's block of council flats, this consists of a small tap-room and another somewhat larger room with waitress service. Despite the rather Spartan furnishings, the atmosphere is pleasant enough.

Taking a left along Wisbyerstrasse at the end of Stahlheimerstrasse, it's only 100 metres or so to **Feierabendklause** (10-22, closed Tue), whose bizarre colour scheme and tatty exterior belie the comfortable pub inside. It has Berliner Pilsator on draught and also offers good, cheap food. Its apparent popularity with the locals means that it can be difficult to find a seat.

Now carry on along Wisbyerstrasse until it meets Schönhauser Allee, where on the corner is **Rennsteig** (10-24), selling Berliner Pils (the sign outside says Engelhardt). The simple pine furniture with which this substantial pub/restaurant has recently been refurbished gives it a cosy welcoming appearance inside.

To return to the city centre, assuming that by now you don't feel like walking it, continue down Schönhauser Allee a few hundred metres and you'll find an U-Bahn station.

Author's notes

I wrote this guide to East Berlin pubs just a couple of months before the fall of the wall. During 1988 and 1989 I had spent a considerable amount of time in the east of the city (Prenzlauer Berg in particular), visiting my future wife. I came to love the crumbling Edwardian splendour around Schönhauser Allee.

The situation this guide describes was to change beyond recognition within a very short period of time. First came a flood of beer from West Germany, decimating the output of all the breweries in the DDR. Privatisation of the brewing industry was conducted with an incompetence that seemed (and arguably was) positively malicious, especially in Berlin.

These are the breweries that were active in East Berlin at the end of 1989:

VEB Berliner Bürgerbräu
VEB Berliner Kindl Brauerei
VEB Brauerei Bärenquell (closed 1994)
VEB Engelhardt Brauerei
VEB Getränkekombinat Berlin (Berliner Pilsner Brauerei, founded 1902; bought 1920 by Kindl and became Berliner Kindl Brauerei Abteilung III; 1945 became a Sovjetischen Aktiengesellschaft (SAG); 1969 became part of Getränkekombinat Berlin; 1990 (or 1991) bought by Brau und Brunnen (Kindl); 199? sold to Schultheiss after Kindl had bought the Potsdamer Rex-Brauerei.
VEB Schultheiss Brauerei Leninallee
VEB Schultheiss Brauerei Schönhauser Allee, Abt. Weissbier (home of the classic Berliner Weisse and the first revived Leipziger Gose)

Where are they now?

John Amer sent me this report on the state of these pubs in early 2005:

> "In your article you didn't put any road numbers in, but I am reasonably certain I didn't miss any pubs. So here goes.
>
> Metzer Eck still there. In some some Berlin tours guide as a good example of a good Kneipe.
>
> Budike 15. If this is number 15 Husemannstrasse, it is now called November and done out in yuppie/ grand cafe style. There also a Irish pub in Husemannstrasse, just called the Irish Pub!
>
> Zum Hackepeter now an Indian Restaurant.
>
> Zum Schusterjungen still there. Front part is still pubby, the back is mainly eating.
>
> Kohlensaure Niederlage unable to find.
>
> Zur Pappel unable to find. [Now called Sergena, Pappelallee 19. R.P.]
>
> Humannklause unable to find.
>
> Braustubl still there. Been refurbished, good back street local.
>
> Feirabendklause unable to find. [I think it's now Mauerblümchen, Wisbyer Str. 4. R.P.]
>
> Rennsteig unable to find. "

Mini Book Series volume XXV: DDR!

III Thuringia in the DDR

Introduction

Thuringia, which now forms the south-western corner of the DDR, consists, approximately, of the 'Bezirk' of Suhl, Erfurt and Gera. Its landscape is dominated by rolling hills and forests, still containing much wildlife, which contrast sharply with the grim, industrial image of the DDR. The Thüringer Wald in the south is an area of particular natural beauty. Only the northeast, in the region of Jena and Gera, is spoilt by the more obtrusive presence of industry. The countryside is dotted with villages of ancient half-timbered houses, seemingly almost untouched by the 20th century. For the most part these are still real living communities rather than groups of city commuters trying to rediscover rural life. Consequently most villages still have a baker's, butcher's and, of course, a pub.

From 1920 to 1952 Thuringia was a 'land' or state (and should be again as of late 1990 when the DDR becomes a federal state) with its capital in Weimar, then later in Erfurt. There are many other attractive towns, some unfortunately wearing their age badly, and most of any reasonable size have a brewery.

Thuringian breweries and beer

Thuringia has a long history as a brewing centre and still boasts one of the largest concentrations of the country's 250 or so breweries. Unsurprising, given that Franconia, with the greatest density of breweries in the world, is just over the border in the Federal Republic. The beers from any given brewery beers are usually only sold in the local area. This admirably decentralised approach does however have the disadvantage that, in any given town, 90% of the pubs sell the same beer. An exception to this are the 'spezial' or 'delikat' beers from certain breweries (such as Apolda or Braugold), which are sold as premium products and tend to be found in posher outlets all over Thuringia. An interesting development as a result of the border being opened, is the appearance, albeit at treble the price of the local stuff, of West German beer in both shops and pubs. A disadvantage of the open border is that you may be competing for pub space with crowds of W. Germans attracted by the, for them, laughably low prices in the DDR.

Beers

The beers are all bottom-fermented, though the Schmitt brewery in the village of Singen produces a pale top-fermenting beer. Most are unpasteurised and the bottled beer will develop a sediment after 6 to 7 days. They fall into the following general categories:

Hell	pale and fairly thin
Pils	with a bit more body, often quite bitter
Pilsator	a bit darker and more like a true Czech Pils
Spezial	a premium Pils, the bottled equivalent of Pilsator
Bock	a winter beer (available November to January) of about 16% Balling - can vary in colour from amber to black

Schwarz	as the name suggests, a dark lager, similar in style to Czech Tmavé Pivo

The Reinheitsgebot has never been enforced in the DDR, originally due to raw material shortages in the 1950's. Currently, the ordinary pils and hell beers are brewed using about 70% malt and the spezial and bock beers using about 80%. Both use about 10% sugar. Despite this, some of the beers, especially the pilsators, are very characterful and compare favourably with some of the rather inoffensive pils-style beers of the Federal Republic. In fact, with their bitter emphasis, the DDR beers are often more reminiscent of the pale Czech lagers. With the availability of W. German beers in the DDR it is now possible to directly compare the products of the two nations' breweries. In Muhlhausen, for example, beer from Eschwege (about 30km away over the border) is on sale. After a couple of glasses of the excellent local Turmquell Pilsator I tried Eschweger Pils which, although as it proudly proclaimed brewed to the Reinheitsgebot, seemed thin and almost tasteless in comparison.

Breweries

The specific beers, by brewery, in the towns described are as follows:

Vereinsbrauerei Apolda

Classic	malty with a strong bitter finish

Eisenacher Brauerei

Hell	a bit thin and watery
Wartburg Pils	sweetish flavour with a bitterish aftertaste
Bock	amber coloured, pleasantly malty

Braugold Erfurt

Pils	a good, clean, very bitter beer
Angerbrau	well-balanced and bitter

J. Andreas Klosterbrauerei, Eschwege, Federal Republic

Eschweger Pils	neutral flavour with a slight bitter aftertaste

Brauerei Gotha

Pils	thin and bitter
Diabetiker	malty aroma and bitter, slightly strange, taste
Spezial	bitter aroma and bitter taste

Brauerei Jena

Pils	light with a bitter aftertaste

Kostritzer Schwarzbierbrauerei, Bad Kostritz

Schwarzbier	Black, fairly sweet and malty

Muhlhausen Turmquell (bottled)

Pils	light, rounded malt aroma and bitter taste
Spezial	hoppy, slightly acidic flavour, with a bitterish finish
Bock	slightly sweet, malty flavour with bitter finish

Muhlhausen Turmquell (draught)

Pils	pale and quite bitter
Pilsator	malty/fruity aroma with strong bitter finish

Brauerei Neunspringe, Worbis

Hell	thin with a slight bitter taste
Pils	a bit more body and a bitter finish
Pilsator	slight malty/fruity aroma with a hop finish

Sternquellbrauerei, Plauen

Pils	thinish but bitter
Plaunator	bitter beer with a malty aroma and bitter/buttery finish
Pilsator	bitter taste with a full spicy, hoppy finish
Bock	sweet and dark with a slight caramel finish

Konsum-Brauerei Weimar-Ehringsdorf

Ehringsdorfer Pils	thin but pleasantly bitter

Exportbier-Brauerei Wernesgrun

Wernesgruner Pils	malty aroma and bitter aftertaste

The companies listed above are all VEB (Volkseigener Betrieb) or nationalised firms (apart from the Eschwege brewery, of course), but, especially in the south, there are still several very small private breweries operating. Examples of these are the Brauerei Göpfert in Jüchsen, Brauerei Geßner in Steinach and Brauerei Schmitt in Singen (the smallest brewery in the DDR). The best bet for finding the beers from these breweries is probably to visit their home village.

A couple of notes on DDR pub etiquette. Everywhere is waiter service only and no standing is allowed. Unfortunately chronic staff shortages (made worse by the recent exodus of many catering personnel to the west) mean that there are often insufficient waiters to serve the whole pub. Hence the 'reserviert' ('reserved') and 'bestellt' ('booked') signs sitting on tables which remain unused all day. It's not unusual for half the tables in a pub to be out of action in this way. It's also not a good idea to start moving chairs around from one table to another without asking, as the waiters often take offence (though the recent surge of visitors from the Federal Republic seems to have helped to loosen them up a little in this respect). All of this can make it difficult to find seats (and hence get a drink), especially for a large group of people. The best way around this is to turn up at an off-peak time (i.e. not 12 - 13 or after 21). Also bear in mind that closing time means what it says - it's when the pub will lock its doors for the night, not last orders. Don't expect to get a drink in the last 15 minutes before closing.

Most pubs and restaurants are run by HO (Handelsorganisation), a state company which runs all types of retail outlets, including shops. The rarer private pubs are generally a little cosier and more personal inside, but have the same low fixed prices as the state enterprises.

Beer prices vary from about .80 M a half litre for hell to around 1.30 M for spezial or bock beers. W. German beer is about 4.00 M a half litre. Meals vary from around 2 - 5 M in a pub to 6 - 15 M in a hotel or posher restaurant. Don't assume that the latter will always assure you higher quality. Often the small and seemingly grotty corner pubs offer much better value in terms of quality and price, though the choice of meals may be limited.

Those intending to travel by rail should note that Deutsche Reichsbahn's services are notoriously slow and unreliable. However, due to the lack of a Dr. Beeching there are still innumerable branch lines, making it possible to reach many quite small villages by rail, as long as you're patient. Most stations of any size have a Mitropa or buffet where hot food and drinks (including draught beer) can be purchased. When in a strange town desperate for a beer but unable to find a pub open, the local Mitropa is usually your best bet. They open seven days a week, from the early morning until 11 or 12 at night. But be warned that it seems to be increasingly difficult to obtain bottled beer in stations, so if you want some refreshment during your journey it's best to buy in a few bottles beforehand. On the main express routes the trains often have Mitropa buffet cars selling simple food and bottled beer. On busier trains, these are good for generating despairingly long queues.

Eisenach

Eisenach, a town crammed into steep, wooded valleys on the road and rail routes between Frankfurt and Leipzig, is a good place to enter the DDR and for me to start a description of a few Thuringian towns. Stuck on one of the hilltops around the town is the picturesque medieval Wartburg castle, where Martin Luther hid out for a while when things got a bit nasty during the Reformation. The castle has also given its name to the car which is the town's main product. The Wartburg plant and various component factories take up big chunks of the town and contribute, along with all the coal fires, to the rather dirty air. The centre of town, with Bach's birthplace (now a museum) and the market place is reasonably attractive. However, the council has seen fit to demolish a large area of old buildings behind the baroque town hall and intends building modern flats there. The town's brewery is at the start of the road leading up to the castle. A large window gives a good view of the copper, but on the whole the place looks ramshackle and in need of renovation.

Like many places in the DDR, the town centre is short on pubs (one of the few, the Marktschanke on the marketplace is closed for an unspecified period of renovation). But don't let this make you despair - just 5 minutes away from the centre there are plenty, if you know where to look.

Starting on one of the main squares in town, Platz Deutsch-Sowjetische-Freundschaft (which may well have changed its name by the time you read this) is the hotel **Thuringer Hof.** When it was built in the days of the German Empire, it must have been modern, fashionable and luxurious. Now its faded opulence is a good backdrop for anyone wishing to play out their Grand Hotel fantasies. The restaurant is still impressive enough, with its oak-panelling and crystal chandeliers, and is an eminently suitable place for those wanting to dine in style without paying accordingly stylish prices. The prices are, however, towards the upper end of the DDR scale. In keeping with its upmarket image, it sells Apoldaer Classic instead of usual Eisenacher Pils, of which you'll soon have had more than enough.

Leaving the square along Johannisstr. and crossing Johannisplatz, just a little up the hill on Frauenberg is **Gaststatte Wartburghof** (Mon, Thu, Sun 15-22; Fri, Sat 15-24; Tue, Wed closed), selling Eisenacher Pils, a cosy private pub of several rooms off a central bar. In both layout and atmosphere it resembles an old Yorkshire corridor pub. Like most of the DDR's private establishments, it has a few more personal decorative touches than the state run HO bars. The beer is served in a wide range of variations on the theme 'straight beer glass'. Some of the glasses, of types not usually seen any more, look ready to take well-earned retirement.

Carrying on up Frauenberg after another small square (which also contains the Bach house) is Rittergasse, on which is **Gasthaus Harmonie** (10 - 18, Tue Wed closed), selling Eisenacher Hell. It's a typical down-to-earth DDR boozer, of the type which seems to act as a substitute factory/school canteen. At lunchtime it's full of schoolkids presenting their school dinner tickets and factory workers tucking into incredibly cheap food served on plastic trays. If you prefer to do your drinking without the company of the local brats, turning up after 13:00 is probably a good idea. Whatever the clientele, the single plain room is always cheerful, friendly and very good value.

Now continue along Friedrich-Engels Straße, an extension of Frauenberg, and in an ornate turn of the century building is **Drachenschlucht** which sells, as almost everywhere else here, Eisenacher Pils. The name, meaning 'dragon's gorge', comes from a glacial feature close by in the Thuringer Wald and there's a beautifully tacky painting of it (complete with dragon, maiden and St. George type) on the wall inside. There are also a couple of barrel ends and jokey cartoons, of the sort beloved by pub decorators the world over, to brighten the place up. Otherwise, it's a fairly middle of the table sort of HO establishment with the usual low, low prices. Thankfully, it doesn't attract the usual big, big crowds of thirsty drinkers.

Mühlhausen

30 km north of Eisenach, just 45 terrifying minutes away along a crumbling and treacherous road (it's not a good idea to try navigating it after dark) is the ancient town of Mühlhausen. If you happen to get thirsty on the way, the village of Mihla has three pubs. Mühlhausen is graced with a virtually complete town wall and, of more practical value, two breweries (one of which is built into said wall). Inside the old fortifications, not a lot has changed in the last few centuries. There's a maze of twisting streets and narrow alleyways all lined with half-timbered buildings leaning at disturbing angles. Unfortunately for the inhabitants, but fortunately for us tourists wishing to recapture the atmosphere of the past, most of the houses don't seem to have been modernised since they were built. A few months ago I would have added that they also didn't seem to have been painted since their construction, but, in honour of the recent influx of guests from over the border, a few of the main streets have seen their facades receive a well-needed lick of

paint. I'm sure that it's dirty, dingy, generally unkempt appearance is far more in keeping with the spirit of the Middle Ages than are the antiseptically tidied and prettied up towns over the border. The town is also famous for the quality and quantity of its bakers. They produce the typical dark German rye bread in hearteningly traditional manner, without the use of the chemical additives so common in the west.

On Görmaer Straße, just inside the wall on the way into town from the railway station, is the **Hotel Grune Linde** (8 - 24), selling the excellent draught Turmquell Pilsator. This is a pub/restaurant of a slightly higher class, so your table will have a tablecloth, albeit probably not very clean. The single large room is comfortable enough and the tables seem happily immune to the plague of 'bestellt' signs (the current record for these is held by the Lindenhof of Eisenach, which one evening contained eight tables, two customers and six 'reserviert' signs). On the walls, no doubt at the whim of an HO interior decorator, hang some arty and enigmatic prints of trees, totally out of keeping with the nature of the place and its customers, who don't exactly look like the type to knock around in art galleries.

Carrying on down Görmaer Straße, one of the streets recently having undergone a slight face-lift, you'll come to Wilhelm-Pieck-Platz. Pretty well directly opposite where you enter the square is the **Mühlhauser Bierbar** (16-23:30; Sat, Sun closed), an unassuming old building without much indication of being a pub. Inside its cramped interior, in the wonderful HO 'heritage' style (pine furniture and obviously designed folksy decoration), a variety of DDR beers are available. The selection varies, but you can usually count on Bad Kostritzer Schwarzbier and Wernesgrüner Pils, both bottled (unfortunately so in the case of the latter, which tastes much better in its unpasteurised draught form). This is the only specialist beer bar in the area and, judging by its popularity, you would think that it was the only pub in the area full stop. A word of advice: arrive closer to 16:00 than 23:30. (If you are unable to get in, nip over the road to the modern Stadt Mühlhausen Hotel, which sells Turmquell Pilsator on draught and stays open until midnight.)

You now have a chance to see the centre of town on the way to your next stop - this saves wasting too much valuable time on sightseeing. On leaving the beer bar, walk to the diagonally opposite corner of the square, up Linsenstr., then left along Herrenstr past the Marienkirche. Through the Frauentor, one of the old town gates and an impressive chunk of stonework, you'll find a fairly desolate piece of open ground. To the right of this, on Johannis Straße, is **Gaststatte Drei Rosen** (10-17; Sat, Sun closed). One glance and the neglected and crumbling plaster of the facade tells you that you're in for a treat and, when you enter, the austerity of the interior is no disappointment. From the rudimentary counter, bare walls and tubular steel furniture of its single square room to the outside toilets (aspiring to Czech standards of filthiness) everything is perfect. It deserves to be preserved in its pristine state as a memorial to the HO minimalist school of pub design. It's to be hoped the changing times won't see such monuments swept away. Your fellow customers are likely to be as straight-forward as the surroundings, but the atmosphere is relaxed and conducive to the quiet enjoyment of a glass or two of the Turmquell Pils which is on offer. A little further along Johannisstr., through another old gate, is the Turmquell bottled beer brewery, some of whose workers you might well rub shoulders with in Drei Rosen.

On leaving turn left, left again into Petristeinweg, then right along Petriteich following the town wall around (another chance for a quick spot of sightseeing here) until reaching Ammerstr. Turn left into here and a couple of hundred metres along, easily spotted by its distinctive green colour-scheme, is the strangely-named **Ammerscher Bahnhof** (10 - 20; Sun, Mon closed). Strangely-named, because not only is there no Ammerscher station in the vicinity, but no station of any description and not even a railway line. Here there's a bit more choice, with Turmquell Pilsator on draught and Gothaer Spezial and Eschweger Pils in bottles. There's a spacious dining area, a small taproom and another small dining room at the back. The higher quality wooden furniture, numerous pot plants and better standard of decoration are dead giveaways that this is a private pub. One wall has a particularly good mural of Muhlhausen, taken from an old engraving. Oddly enough, despite the visible outward signs of comfort, there's a lack of warmth in the surroundings. The grotty and Spartan Drei Rosen is actually a far more welcoming spot in which to enjoy a glass of beer and a quiet conversation. In just the same way that your local public bar is more convivial than a Berni Inn. In many respects, Ammerscher Bahnhof resembles more a W. German pub and I suppose that the cooler atmosphere goes along with that. They also use handled mugs instead of the usual straight glasses, a suspicious practice if I ever saw one, and the ceiling has fake beams.

Schlotheim

Fifteen kilometers north-east of Mühlhausen, reached either by road or a single-track branch line, is the small town of Schlotheim. Again, the impatient ones amongst you can refresh themselves on the way in the village of Korner, which has a Gaststatte in an attractive old detached building.

In Schlotheim itself is the **Schloß Gaststatte** (10-22; Fri, Sat 10-24; Mon closed), a baroque palace dating from 1772 which has been converted into a community centre. The palace was built on the foundations of an older, fortified castle, of which you can see traces, and is still surrounded by a dry moat. One section of the building is used as a restaurant, containing three diversely and surprisingly pleasantly decorated rooms. The first, the Bauernstube (farmer's room) is in rustic style with plain wooden furniture. The second is more like a standard restaurant. The third, the Spiegelzimmer (mirror room), is in a palatial baroque style with ornate furniture, chandeliers and, of course, whole walls of mirrors. All in all, the conversion has been very well done, making it stylish and interesting, without being at all intimidating. It's used mostly by locals and is surprisingly uncrowded. Try to visit before the W. Germans discover it and spoil all of that.

Leinefelde

30 km north of Muhlhausen, on the edge of the Eichsfeld, an exposed and intemperate hilly area, is Leinefelde. Formerly a large village, it became a town in 1969 with the development of a local textile industry. The town reflects this, having a relatively small centre of typically Thuringian houses, surrounded by large estates of mid-rise flats.

On the main street, at the opposite end of town to the railway station, is the **Eichsfelder Hof** (10 - 23; Sun closed). Housed in a large detached building next to the Catholic church (the Eichsfeld is one of the few Roman Catholic areas of the DDR), its expansive interior contains numerous rooms. Downstairs are a basic taproom in the Czech plain pine style and a more comfortable restaurant. Upstairs are various function rooms. Usually available are draught Neunspringe Pils and bottled Braugold Angerbrau Pils. Draught Wernesgruner Pils has also been known to make an appearance here, but you'll have to be on particularly good terms with the waiter to get a taste of it, as it's kept for the regulars.

On the Centraler Platz, a modern shopping precinct that immediately conjures up images of Hounslow, Peterlee, or Corby, is the inspiringly-named **Stadt Leinefelde** restaurant (10 - 18; Sat, Sun closed). From the outside it looks like a 60's community centre, but once inside this image is immediately dispelled - it's more like a school assembly hall set out with tables for an examination. Large, modern - in the most depressing architectural meaning of the word - and Spartan, it's not outwardly the most welcoming place to go for a meal. However the food is good and cheap and the service excellent, as this is where trainee catering staff receive their practical experience. The beer, Braugold Pils, is also top class.

Gotha

30 km east of Eisenach, along the main railway line and the motorway, is Gotha. It's another typical larger Thuringian town, many of whose attractive half-timbered are in dire need of tarting up. From the 1640's the Archdukes of Sachsen-Gotha had their residence here in an imposing Baroque palace, the Schloß Friedenstein. Stuck on top of a hill between the railway station and the centre, the castle and its gardens dominate the town. From it, there's a good view over the red tile roofs of the houses around the old market. Along Bahnhofstr., which leads logically enough from the station to the town centre, are monuments to another group of the town's past inhabitants: the 19th century bourgeoisie. The street is lined with substantial stone villas now, somewhat ironically, used as offices by VEB companies and socialist organisations. Sadly, this is another town whose council was a bit too eager in using bulldozers to solve its renovation problems.

GOTHAER PILS

DEUTSCHES PILSNER

HSL 1823600
Lagertemperatur 5–8°C

VOLLBIER
VEB Brauerei Gotha
im VEB Getränkekombinat Erfurt

0,5 l

0,92 M

0,33 l

0,61 M

Right in the centre of town, on the Hauptmarkt, is Turiec, a complex of a cafe and a couple of restaurants. One of these is Slovan, offering excellent Slovak cuisine. The recently refurbished interior is one of the more comfortable and tasteful examples of the HO 'heritage' stripped pine style. The food is slightly more expensive than average, but well worth it. The beer served is Apoldaer Classic. Borovicka, the Slovak version of gin, is also available.

Going from the sublime to the ridiculous, my next recommendation is the **Mitropa** (10 - 22) in the Hauptbahnhof. Even in a country where pubs rate on a scale of basic, very basic or incredibly basic, this is an establishment of exceptionally low class. Housed in a portacabin hidden away, as if even Deutsche Reichsbahn were ashamed of it, at the end of a platform, its contents have been stripped down to the barest essentials. It makes you feel lucky that they remembered to include chairs. Despite all of this, it isn't without a certain charm and is certainly very good value. Thankfully, it isn't full of the non-travelling, obnoxious drunks which plague some of the Mitropas in larger cities (notably Leipzig, where you look out of place if you enter sober and carrying luggage). In keeping with the minimalist approach, it's also self-service.

Erfurt

Carrying on another 25 km east of Gotha is the Bezirk town of Erfurt, the largest city in Thuringia. It's also the only major city in the DDR which wasn't totally flattened by bombing during the war. As a result, it retains an attractive old centre, including the unusual Kramerbrucke, a bridge covered in half-timbered houses. The town contains a good mixture of medieval, renaissance and neo-gothic architecture, reflecting its long history as a cultural and political centre. The Dom and Severikirche, next door to each other on a hill, are particularly imposing, especially from the massive square below them.

On this square, directly facing the two churches, is an unassuming little pub (whose name unfortunately escapes me). I do recall, however, that it's a plain beer-hall type place with long, rough wooden tables. On the walls are some very interesting blue and white tile murals depicting the history of the town. For its central location it's remarkably un-touristy and uncrowded - probably because of its unprepossessing exterior and basic interior. This makes it very useful, as the centre isn't exactly overflowing with boozers to choose from. It also serves a very nice glass of the distinctive Braugold Pils.

On the way to the railway station, on Bahnhofstr., is **Burgerhof**, a sizeable restaurant with a modern interior. With its angular metallic furniture and strident decor, it's unselfconsciously ugly in the way of a 1960's cafeteria. The staff's eagerness to sprinkle around the 'bestellt' signs can make it difficult to get in. The reward if you do is more of the wonderful Braugold Pils.

Actually opposite the main station on Bahnhofplatz in the grand **Erfurter Hof** hotel is the Pilsner beer bar. A single room reached its furnished in the decorator's imagination of a Czech beer hall - that is: barrels for tables and lots of wood everywhere. Still, the beer is at least the genuine article. Pilsner Urquell. Downstairs the hotel has a very posh baroque restaurant, which is good to try if you can't find anywhere else to eat. The menu is more interesting and imaginative than is usual in the DDR and the service pretty good. Expect to pay for this, with prices at the very top of the scale. This sells Braugold Angerbrau Pils in bottles.

Over the other side of Bahnhofplatz in the **Mitropa** (9 - 23) you can experience the opposite extreme of the DDR culinary world. A cavernous self-service buffet, where the food comes on those very classy plastic trays with little hollows for each different dish. Basic, but not rough, its good value and handy if you're in a rush. Again, you can treat yourself to some Braugold Pils.

Weimar

Another 25 km east of Erfurt is Weimar, a city associated in British minds with the decadence of 20's Germany (which in fact mostly took place in Berlin). To Germans, it's one of the main centres of classical German culture through its connections with Goethe, Schiller and a host of other writers, musicians and painters. In one of those little ironies of 30's Germany, one of the most notorious concentration camps, Buchenwald, is just outside this city of art. Today they concentrate on the more cultured aspects of the past and the town is littered with museums and memorials to Goethe and Schiller. The centre of the town, having been spared bombing, is very attractive. In keeping with its prominence in the 18th and 19th centuries, there's a higher proportion of neo-classical architecture than elsewhere in Thuringia.

On Markt, smack in the centre of the old town, is the **Hotel Elephant**. Its cellar restaurant (10 - 22), recently tarted up, has the vaulted ceiling and appearance typical of a Ratskellar. It possibly verges a little on the bland, with little decoration and rather glaring lighting. The food is pretty good and not too unreasonable in price. The beer is draught Ehringsdorfer Pils. Walking over to the opposite side of the Markt and along Dimitroffstrasse you come to another square, Herderplein. Here is **Gastmahl des Meeres**, the local branch of a chain of fish restaurants. They vary in quality (the one opposite the Fernsehturm in Berlin is to be avoided), but this is one of the better ones. In its uncomplicated single room, decked out in appropriately nautical style, there's a good range of seafood at very reasonable prices. Again, the beer is Ehringsdorfer Pils.

Jena

Continuing eastward from Weimar another 25 km will bring you to Jena, a town made famous by the Karl Zeiss optical works (and the football team of the same name). Its impact on the town is very evident as, although the town has a long history and a famous university, the factory dominates the town, covering a large central area. The rest of the town looks rather down-at- heel, with the extensive war damage not particularly well repaired. The Marktplatz has been restored, but otherwise there's just the odd original building stuck between a collection of banal post-war constructions. A bit like Frankfurt-am-Main, on a smaller scale.

On Lutherplatz, between the Hauptbahnhof and the city centre is the **Schwarzer Bär**. This modest old building is, remarkably, the only hotel in town (unbelievable, given that it has a population of over 100,000). The small and homely restaurant (10 - 22) has a limited but ample range of food and sells the local Jena Pils on draught.

Over on the other side of town is Westbahnhof. Looking remarkably like a rural station in the UK, this houses one of the few genuinely pleasant and welcoming **Mitropas** (10 - 22). It's compact and cosy, without the appearance of having changed a great deal since the station was built. Perhaps its slightly obscure location and branch line character save it from the unsavoury characters who tend to plague Mitropas. It sells draught Jena Pils.

Plauen

I II III IV V VI VII VIII IX X XI XII

SBP

TGL 7764
INHALT 0,33 l

HSL 1823 100
INHALT 0,5 l

III-6-15

0,48 M   hell   VOLLBIER   0,72 M

VEB STERNQUELLBRAUEREI PLAUEN
IM VEB GETRÄNKEKOMBINAT KARL-MARX-STADT

1   3   5   7   9   11   13   15   17   19   21   23   25   27   29   31

60 km to the southeast of Jena is Plauen, a town which is not in fact in Thuringia but just over the border in Sachsen. It's capital of the Vogtland, a windswept area of deep valleys straddling Thuringia and Sachsen just to the north of the Czech border. The scenery and buildings are very different, more reminiscent of those in northern Czechoslovakia. A little of the Czech influence also seems to have rubbed off on the beer, which is very good. Plauen itself, despite heavy war damage, has an attractive and relaxed city centre. The town gives an impression of greater size than its population of 80,000 would indicate, probably because it was once much larger. Before the First World War it had over 120,000 inhabitants. On the Altmarkt is the fine late-Gothic Rathaus, which has been very well restored. The city's trams are also of note, having been given over to various groups to decorate. This makes for some colourful and interesting sights clattering through the streets, quite unusual for the DDR. One in particular is very sweet, being decked out in lace curtains (lace is the most famous local product). It's like travelling through town in your grandmother's front room.

A tram ride out of the centre, at Reusaerstr. 84, is **Erlers Restaurant** (15 - 23; Mon, Tue closed). This old and once run down corner pub, now private, attracts the young and trendy of Plauen, but don't let that put you off. The interior is still old-fashioned and welcoming. It avoids both the Spartan steel or heritage pine styles of HO places and the cold plushness of some private pubs. It has two fair-sized rooms, panelled in wood, with wooden floors and old coal stoves. The walls, painted in a comforting, if strange, shade of dark green, are covered in shelves stuffed with a collection of old bottles and other bits and bobs. In short, a proper pub, of the type with which the UK used to be filled before the brewers started their improvements. It sells pizzas, which, if not exactly authentic, make a reasonably inexpensive and filling snack. On sale is the tasty Sternquell Pilsator, another very drinkable beer.

Back more in the centre of town **Zum Bären** (7 - 23) at Wilhelm-Pieckstr. 38 and **Gruner Kranz** (Mon 16-22; Thu, Fri 16-24; Wed 11-19:30) are two more conventional HO pubs, both selling Sternquell Pils.

IV Eisenach Pub Guide

Introduction

Eisenach is a town which will always have a special place in my heart, for a multiplicity of reasons. For one, it's where I was married (and the authorities thoughtfully sent along someone to photograph the proceedings, without us even having to ask). It's also a rather charming old place, which despite its many important historical associations, is oddly unknown in the English-speaking world.

Here is a quick crash course in the town's significance:

Bach was born here
it has one of Germany's most impressive medieval castles, Wartburg
it's here (in Wartburg castle) that Martin Luther first translated the bible into German
it was home to the world-renowned Wartburg car factory (it wasn't exactly well-known for the right reasons)

The old town is a significant size and mostly quite well preserved. A few bits on the edge were left to rot then replaced by Plattenbau, but the rest hasn't been fiddled with too much in the last century. Sadly, some of the villas on the Wartburg side of town have been standing empty for years as arguments rage as to who exactly the legal owner is. It has, ironically, caused many similar problems to the ones arising from lack of investment from the DDR authorities - fine buildings crumbling slowly to rubble.

On the west east side of town there's a chunk of the old city wall slicing across Georgenstrasse. But it's nothing that would keep out an agile 5-year old, let alone rampaging Austian/Bavarian/Prussian armies. The only even vaguely convincing section is Karlstor (Karl's Tower), gateway to the town's first significant square, Karlsplatz (formerly Platz der Deutsch-Sowjetischen Freundschaft). The square is one of many spots in Eisenach of which I have eternal recollections. Not many wedding parties leave the reception by bus, but it was a pleasure accorded us. Our own very special wedding bendy-bus left from Platz DSF.

You can criticise the DDR regime for many things, but their stance on drink-driving couldn't be faulted. The legal limit for alcohol in the blood was effectively nil and the penalties (jail sentences in many cases) certainly acted as a deterrent to irresponsible behaviour. No drunken guest stupid enough to drive us home, no taxi to be found (check out the difference now - whole caravans at every taxi stand); what else can you do but take the bus? It looks very romantic in "The Graduate", bride in wedding dress (to be perfectly accurate, jilting bride in the film). Standing amongst the shoppers in our ill-fitting suits (in my wife's case, beautiful white dress) was a far more prosaic experience. Well, it would have been, if Dave hadn't spotted the kiosk just by the bus stop.

You can criticise the DDR regime for many things, but the general availability of alcoholic drinks, in all strengths, under their government couldn't be faulted. Quicker than you could say "we're a bunch of alcoholics" we were all supplied with miniatures, proper Nordhäuser, I think. The journey was an event for my British guests, not only because of the novelty of riding in an articulated bus.

To return from the world of nostalgia to the more urbane one of disseminating information; here is one tip for you all. I found a little free booklet called "Gastronomischer Stadtbummel: Eiseneach und Umgebung" of great help. It's in both English and German, which is very thoughtful. You should be able to pick it up at a hotel or the tourist office:

Tourist Information
Markt,
99817 Eisenach.
Tel.: 03691 - 7923-0, 03691 - 19433
Fax: 03691 - 792320
Email: tourist-info@www.eisenach.de
Homepage: http://www.eisenach.de/

Opening times: Mon: 10:00 - 18:00
Tue-Fri: 09:00 - 18:00
Sat-Sun: 10:00 - 14:00

Eisenach, its Beer, its Pubs

Eisenacher Brauerei

In the town is the mid-sized (40,000 hl a year) Eisenacher Brauerei. It's very central, on the big avenue that leads from town towards Wartburg castle. Some of is rustically half-timbered, some industrial late 19th century brick and you can see through big display windows to some of the coppers. There were a few lorries hanging about, but I couldn't see much else going on. Maybe I was there on a slow day.

I've drunk beer from the brewery since 1987. In the early days, it was OK. The Helles was a bit thin. Wartburg Pils was drinkable, but very unstable. If properly (and quickly) tapped, it was quite a reasonable beer. Bottled, you needed to buy it and drink it straight away. If you walked slowly, it could go sour before got home. Perhaps hygiene wasn't all it could have been inside the brewery.

After 1989, beer flooded in from the West and sales plummeted. The local pub trade stayed loyal enough to keep the brewery going. After a refit of the brewhouse, the beer quality has improved tremendously. Sales seem to have picked up and the Wartburg trademark to be of some value again (I don't think the make of car with the same name did it much good). Their beers aren't the best in the world, but they're reasonable and certainly above average for the area. They also produce a fair range of styles - Pils, Export, Bock, Schwarzbier - though the Helles, once their mainstay in the off-trade, has disappeared. (Helles in general, has had a poor time of it in the old DDR since re-unification.)

Their dark lager, Schwarzer Drachen is an interesting beer. Introduced in the 90's to take advantage of the popularity of Köstritzer Schwarzbier, it has changed its taste over the years. Initially quite sweet, it's now very much in the current trend of the style - dry and with quite a bit of malt bitterness. It's odd to see a style becoming bitterer these days.

Eisenach Pubs

There have been many pub closures in the time I have known Eisenach, but it's still got a perfectly respectable number for a town of its population. I've found listings for over 70 licensed premises to serve the 45,000 inhabitants. The variation in drinking establishments is good: Bavarian beerhalls, cosy pubs, traditional restaurants, local bars.

I found that the standard of pubs was generally high. That there were plenty of cosy, traditional places around. It's probably because, having been done out in the last ten years, they missed out on all the horrible design disasters of the 70's and 80's. My only observation, though this could well have been because of me visiting at early hours, was that there appeared a shortage of customers. I was there outside tourist season, too, so this is most likely total crap that I've just written. No doubt in Summer you'll be driven crazy by the crowds.

The overwhelming majority of pubs, to my great admiration, still get their standard draught beers from the local Eisenach brewery. Wartburg Pils and Schwarzer Drachen are on most bars and why not? They usually offer beers from elsewhere too. It's only right that in a small town the local brewery should provide the standard beer. Sadly, there are many towns in Germany, especially in the East, where this is not the case.

Augustiner and Paulaner from Munich both have tied pubs in the town. You'll also find beer from other Bavarian breweries - notably Kulmbacher and Tucher. Products from nearby parts of the East - Köstritzer, Radeberger and Sternquell - mean that you can obtain an unusual mixture of beers in the town. Things are just slowly reverting to how they were before Germany was divided. Bavaria isn't a great distance away and their large brewers must always have has a presence here.

Personal Memories

To the left you can see the Lindenhof, which is currently on the market and I am sure will be attracting the attention of astute investors everywhere. Here is one of the many locations in Eisenach that conjure up

very personal memories.

It may look a wreck now, but in 1988 it was totally different - all the windows had glass and there was draught beer. Inspirational design and sophistication weren't words that cropped up the HO's mission statement. Lindenhof took this corporate philosophy to the absolute limit. Today it's possible to peep at the bar inside through some of the smashed boards and, despite the vandalism, it's not looking that much worse than when I last had a beer there in 1988. The outside hasn't deteriorated considerably, either. It looks as if someone might have even tidied up the garden since the old days.

If you're thinking that's the grip this pub has on my throat and mind, then you're very wrong. The memory that will never fade from my mind emanates from my wedding feast. Over the road at my in-laws house, we were having an after-reception party. A half dozen of my friends and family were staying there for a few days around the wedding. My father-in-law had bought in a barrel of Wartburg Pils, but was worried that we would never get through it. Early in the evening of the wedding day, we had just finished off the second barrel of Wartburg (ordered in emergency after the first had run out after two days).

Lindenhof was just over the road and the only pub in the district open at that time of day. Great idea - we nip over there and buy a couple of crates of beer. After all, this is the DDR and the price of a crate in a pub is the same as in a supermarket. Even in a country where I had learnt to love the charming drabness of the surroundings, Lindenhof was drably charmless. The landlord - a scruffy, miserable git in the best tradition of publicans totally unsuited for their profession - soon disappointed us: they had no bottled beer.

About the only drinks available were draught pils and doppelkorn (and I suppose tap water, though I wouldn't have bet my left shoe on them having running water that was drinkable). What a dilemma: beer a mere 50 metres away from a happy group of revellers, but nothing to transport it in. Suddenly someone - I can't remember who, but he was a man of genius - suggested we fetch a bucket and put 10 litres of draught beer in it.

Now, bar staff could be a fickle bunch in the DDR. Moving a chair from one table to another could be considered as a capital offence. I was once scolded by a waitress for reading a book at the table. Yet being asked to pull 20 beers and tip them into a bucket was seen as a perfectly reasonable request. If you want to appreciate what I mean by this, try doing the same in your local pub. Go in with a bucket and ask them to fill it with beer. I bet you that they won't act as nonchalantly as this bloke did.

Pub Listings

Altdeutsche Bierstube

Alexanderstr 8,
99817 Eisenach.
Tel. 03691 - 732003
Fax:
Homepage:

Opening hours: Mon-Sun 10:00 - open end
Number of draught beers: 3
Number of bottled beers:
Regular draught beers:

Wartburg Pils
Köstritzer Schwarzbier
Radeberger Pils

Food: Snacks €2-5, meals €5-7, beer €2.40 0.5l.
The Bierstube is one of Eisenach's oldest pubs though, hidden away on a side street, you're unlikely to stumble upon it by accident. It has two rooms: the first very much a taproom, behind it is a restaurant.

Cosy may be a cliché, but that is the best word to describe the atmosphere. There are plenty of traditional feature - a Kachelofen (enclosed coal oven), delightful old panelling, a beamed ceiling and wonderful carved columns. Most of the added decoration is beer related, mostly connected with Radeberger or Köstritzer.

Any pub that has a well-entrenched line of middle-aged guys at the bar has to have the word "local" pop up somewhere in its description. They were very keen on the Radeberger. It could be a subconscious effect on people of that age of the product's former rarity. Or they could just prefer it to the Wartburg and I can't say that I could put up too much of an argument against them.

Though one of the reasons for the continued existence of the Eisenacher brewery, which survived the dark days after re-unification, is the loyalty of the local pub trade. When western beers flooded the shops, enough of the landlords kept faith with the town's brewery to keep it going.

Pride in the produce of your local area is a quality that I have always admired. It's one of the many good attitudes of the French. You find it a lot in Germany, too. Around re-unification the former DDR had a bit of an identity crisis. Appreciation of the local specialities (which were mostly available all through the communist time) has returned

and deservedly so. No-one would ever believe me when I said that the best bread and sausage in Germany was to be found in Thuringia. The beer was usually pretty good, too. I still swear (and my brother will too) that Mühlhäuser Pilsator was one of the best beers I've had in the true Pilsner Urquell style (so not pils - not that stuff that has the colour of urine - a beer with a bit of colour and body, so some maltiness as well as a good finish of hops. The style - pilsator - has very, unfortunately, not outlived the SED.
Rating: **** Public transport:

Augustiner Bräu Spezialausschank

Georgenstr 30,
99817 Eisenach.
Tel. 03691 - 215250
Fax: 03691 - 215250
Email: andreasgutsell@arcor.de
http://www.augustiner-eisenach.de/

Opening hours: Mon-Sun 11:00 - 24:00
Number of draught beers: 4
Number of bottled beers: 5
Regular draught beers:

    Augustiner Pils
    Augustiner Lagerbier Hell
    Augustiner Dunkel
    Augustiner Edelstoff

Food: Snacks €3-6, meals €6-14, beer €2.50-2.70 for 0.5l.
As you can tell from the name, this is effectively a tied outlet of Munich's Augustiner brewery. And there's absolutely nothing wrong with that, Augustiner being the pick of the big industrial breweries. It's on the edge of the town centre, about due West of the Markt.

Now my memory may be deceiving me, but I seem to remember, during the late 1980's, spotting a building with a plaster sign from a Munich brewery. I have a definite feeling that it was this pub. I thought: "that's a tied house they'll never get back" - how wrong I was.

Inside you've got yourself a typical traditional Bavarian beerhall, albeit on a relatively small scale. The walls are panelled, the floors wooden and the tables topped with pine. There are plenty of old Augustiner posters (they produced some particularly striking ones in the 20's and 30's) and steins to give the appropriate beery atmosphere. It's all been done with a good deal of taste and has created a old-fashioned, cosy boozer whose young age it would be impossible to guess. A genuine addition to the town and better than any pub they used to have.

The main bar is L-shaped, with the short side along the street, which is faced by the bar counter. There are a couple of other rooms used for functions. It's another one of those pubs that stretch back so far that the restricted frontage on the street can be very deceptive.

The beer selection may be small and bizarrely (perhaps my German isn't as good as I thought and the waitress misinterpreted my question) includes no bottles, but there is Edelstoff, one of my all-time favourite Spezial style beers. The food is a mixture of Bavarian and Thuringian dishes - not a bad combination if you don't have too many waistline issues.

Rating: **** Public transport:

Hotel "Am Bachhaus"

Marienstrasse 7,
99817 Eisenach.
Tel. 03691 - 20470
Fax: 03691 - 2047 133
Email: amBachhaus@oal.com
Homepage: http://www.hotel-am-bachhaus.de/

Opening hours: Mon-Sun 11:00 - 23:00
Number of draught beers: 2
Number of bottled beers:
Regular draught beers:

Eisenacher Schwarzer Drachen
Tucher Pils

Food: Snacks €7-9, meals €8-12.
This hotel, restaurant, pub and probably a few other things as well is just around the corner from where Mr. and Mrs. Bach used to live. You can still see "Johann S rools OK" scratched crudely into the wall of the local bus shelter. I think that 300 years is plenty long enough for the council to have got around to repainting it.

You know when you're in Eisenach's "Bach quarter" (young Johann's graffiti aside) because suddenly all the signposts for pedestrians are multilingual German/Japanese. On a small square (though it's still a street) a little to the South of the Markt, you'll find Am Bachhaus.

Forgive me if I now lapse into my rather dull explanation mode. On entry, ignoring the reception directly opposite you, if you turn left you'll come into the taproom. This is a square room directly behind the front window, and has much of its space occupied by a

U-form bar. Most of the seating here is of the relaxing barstool variety. (My wife refuses to sit on the things, saying they make her legs go numb. The times I've wished that the same thing could happen to my brain, when I'm in some crappy pub - but I almost forgot, isn't that why beer was invented?) But I digress, if we take a small stroll towards the rear, then we'll pass through a series of larger restaurant and function rooms.

The style is what I call "postwar German brewery tap". Out in the forest, another few hectares of pine have felt the axe. A lorry-load of red tiles have been carefully laid. There's not really much about the concept that you can fault. I've been in such places from Düsseldorf to Munich, via Cologne and Stuttgart. Even the cleverest designer can't provide genuine ageing. You can fake it, you can buy it by the yard and lay it out, but it will never be the real thing. The real thing (a cosy, old-fashioned pub) evolves over decades or even centuries. You start off with a basic idea, then just let time take its course: things break, junk accumulates, fag smoke gets deposited. There's no way to get this effect overnight (not convincingly - see the Kartoffelhaus below). Here, they've got the basic material for a very pleasant pub. With loving care, it could be somewhere to delight my grandchildren. Perhaps if "Bomber" ("Butcher" or "War-criminal" would be a more appropriate epithet) Harris hadn't been quite so conscientious in finding German towns that would burn nicely, there would be more unspoilt old pubs.

There's seating for a couple of hundred, but at the unfashionably early time of my visit, I was their only customer. So, as to the nature of the usual clientèle, your guess is as good as mine. But - I'm going out on a limb here - it wouldn't surprise me if the odd hotel guest popped in.

I'm sorry, but being the only person in the joint, there weren't a great number of bar staff around whom I could ask. OK, I admit it: I did forget to enquire about the bottled beers. An informed guess would be the Tucher wheat beers.
Rating: ***   Public transport:

Hotel Glockenhof

Grimmelgasse 4,
99817 Eisenach.
Tel. 03691 - 2340
Fax: 03691 - 234 131
Email: info@glockenhof.de
Homepage:
http://www.glockenhof.de/

Opening hours: Mon-Sun 08:00 - 01:00
Number of draught beers: 4
Number of bottled beers: 4
Regular draught beers:

Wartburg Pils
Köstritzer Schwarzbier
Radeberger Pils
Wernesgruner Pils

Food: Snacks €3-5, meals €5-11, beer €1.60-2.10 0.3l.
If ever a declaration of interest needed were needed, then that time is now. On this spot, we celebrated my wedding reception and it will, accordingly, always (or at least until my wife finally loses her patience with my irresponsibility) evoke within me unique associations. You've been warned - don't expect Mister Rational to remain within the auditorium for the duration of these paragraphs.

Then again, I wouldn't have recognised it if my father-in-law hadn't pointed it out to me as he drove me into town. "Now, we'll have to go down this way, mate, 'cos of the *ing one-way system in this *ing town. See that place there, gov? That's where we 'ad the knees-up after you tied the knot, if I 'member it right." (My pathetic attempt at argot is only my silly, inadequate my way to convey the spirit of the moment. The fact that he really is a taxi-driver is of no relevance here. (My god, he is the bloke who drove me to the Schmitt brewery in Singen, an act for which I will never forget him.) Memory is a fickle friend. I recognised countless other personally totally meaningless landmarks in Eisenach, yet this very significant place sparked not the slightest flicker of memory. My mind must have been on other things at the time.

Now where were we? I was about to launch into my second apology, which is for forgetting to photograph the exterior. I have a good reason for this, in pretty well all circumstances other than these. You wouldn't believe how many photos I take in the course of this gruelling research. Even so, there are occasions on which I need to be economical with the film stock. So I've got into the habit of taking the exterior shot upon exit rather than before entry. There are many dangers inherent in this approach: the light conditions deteriorating whilst inside; not being conscious when leaving; forgetting.

My usual reason for the delay in snapping away is fear of disappointment. How many photos sit sadly in my albums of pubs, unreported in these pages, who let me down. From the outside everything looks good, so, whip out the camera, push the button and rush inside. How similar, as Swiss Tony says, this experience is to "making love to a beautiful woman". These chastising images of a charming appearance harbouring corruption within, haunt every visit to my archive. Traumatised by these experiences, I have become accustomed to capturing the wonderful pictures which grace these pages after leaving, when I'm certain that we're talking about high class broad and not low-rent hooker.

After all this prologue are you still reading? Do you care what this very special hotel/restaurant/pub looks and feels like? I can't say that I'm not tempted to tell you nothing at all. To let you peruse the pics (sadly lacking one of the most vital) and come to your own conclusions. But what is the point in me making all the effort to produce these pages, if I can't force my bigoted and ill-founded opinions down your throats? If you want to see how the exterior looks, the photo on the hotel's homepage is better than I could have managed, anyway.

A lot has changed here since my brother gave his best man's speech. In those days it was a hospice (a sort of cheap hotel/restaurant, not the last resting place of the terminally ill) owned by the protestant church. That's the half-timbered bit on the corner. The restaurant is still retained in (as much as my irritating memory can recall) its original form. The lump adjoining it is the hotel/bistro built when, as a weird side-effect of privatisation, church property got sold off, too. You couldn't build anything with even the vaguest of pretensions to hipness that didn't have a whiff of post-modernism, so on the outside that's what you get.

The new appearance had me fearing the worst. But I was sadly disappointed in my lack of disappointment with the interior. The bistro is (as you can see above) rather swish but at the same time has a real sense of place, mostly through the thoughtful use of old photographs. Bastards. Why couldn't you make a real pig's ear of it? For goodness sake, almost everywhere else in the world they can manage disastrous conversions/extensions/renovations. How come they didn't manage here? The designer must have studied in the East - where they taught trades properly.

The beers? Well, nothing too out of the ordinary. Three of the draught beers are pils, but, if you want a quick guide to former-DDR pils beers, this could be a fair crash course. Bottled they've got Eisenacher Schwarzer Drachen and the set of Franziskaner wheat beers.

There's a beer garden at the back, by the way. And it's a hotel. Of course. Looks pretty nice, too, but you would have to check their website for prices. I would suggest haggling: the major tourist sources - the USA and Japan - are running dry at present, causing a bit of a draught in the hotel trade.
Rating: **** Public transport:

Marktschänke

Markt 19,
99817 Eisenach.
Tel. 03691 - 203 461
Fax:

Opening hours: Mon-Sun 09:30
- open end

Number of draught beers: 3
Number of bottled beers: 4
Regular draught beers:

Wartburg Pils
Eisenacher Schwarzer Drachen
Radeberger Pils

Food: Snacks €4-8, meals €7-10, beer €2.80 0.5l..
It isn't only going to be the Einstein's amongst you who will be able to guess that this pub is on the market place. It is, strangely, about the only straightforward hostelry on the square.

Once inside, it's surprisingly diminutive given the width of the frontage. The chunky pine furniture (I always thought of it as the HO rustic style) looks like it has been kept over from the DDR days. But chaps, that dark green panelling, believe me; it doesn't do the place any favours. It looks as if they've let a four year old pick the colour scheme. And that's a four year old who can't name the colours correctly yet. And had obviously chosen the paint by words. This can be great fun to observe but, believe me, has limited charm.

You can't help thinking that they're not really making the most out of what they've got here. They've got a great spot, you would need to have pretty poor eyesight not to notice it. It's not pubby enough for hanging around in. I think that that with a bit better layout, they could be on a winner. Note the typical design of the older buildings in the town: the outer door opens onto a corridor, from which another door lead into the pub. Couldn't have been keen on draughts.

There are two rooms- a tiny one by the entrance which joins onto a second deeper room, with the bar counter at the rear. Behind the pub there is a small beer garden.
Rating: ***   Public transport:

Gasthof "Am Storchenturm"

Georgenstraße 43a,
99817 Eisenach.
Tel. 0700 - 4040 4050
Fax: 03691 - 733 265
eMail   info@gasthof-am-
storchenturm.de
Homepage: http://www.gasthof-am-
storchenturm.de

Opening hours: Mon-Sun 11:00 -
23:00
Jan-Apr Mon-Fri 11:00 - 23:00, Sat-
Sun 11:00 - 23:00
Number of draught beers: 3
Number of bottled beers: 4
Regular draught beers:

Wartburg Pils
Eisenacher Schwarzer Drachen
Wernesgruner Pils

Food: Snacks €4-8, meals €6-12, beer €2.50 0.5l..
This place had me, even armed with a very useful map showing its location, struggling to find it. My advice is, look for the public library on Georgenstraße, go around the back of it and there, amidst remnants of the city fortifications, you will discover a half-timbered barn. Part of a farm that predates the founding of the town in 1150, it reopened as a pub in 1987. If you pass the thing with the gothic tower in the photo to the left, then you've gone too far and are headed into the uncharted (for me at least) western outreaches of town.

Its name is taken from part of the wall close by, the "Storchenturm", whose roof used to house a stork's nest. Though there's not that much of the tower left nowadays, so didn't have romantic visions of gothic towers. You still can't fault the spot, fronted by a shady beer garden and shielded from the road by neighbouring buildings.

Inside, the half-timbering is still visible, though the rest of the décor is fairly neutral and modern. Some halters and other examples of agricultural retro are sprinkling around just to make sure that you don't forget this was once a barn. OK, I've got the idea. A simple sign saying "ex-barn" would suffice.

The beer list is the same as that of a great many pubs: Wartburg/"luxury pils"/Tucher Weizen beers.
Rating: *** Public transport:

"Das total verrückte Kartoffelhaus"

Sophienstrasse 44,
99817 Eisenach.
Tel. 03691 - 732 626
Fax: 03691 - 785 381
e-mail:
totalverrueckt@Kartoffelhaus.com
Homepage:
www.kartoffelhaus.com/gaeste/esa/

Opening hours: Mon-Sun 11:00 - 14:30 & 17:30 - 01:00
Sun 11:00 - 01:00
Number of draught beers: 4
Number of bottled beers: 2
Regular draught beers:

Sternquell Pils
Kulmbacher Pils
Mönchshof Premium Schwarzbier
Kapuziner Heffeweizen Hell

Food: Snacks €4-8, meals €8-20, beer €2.20 0.5l.
Before you start thinking that I've become a total hypocrite and am now promoting theme outlets, I will give you my reasons for including this particular establishment. It has a handy central location and some tasty beers that I didn't find anywhere else in the town. Will that do?

I felt obliged to give some sort of explanation before divulging that this is one of a chain of potato-dish based pubs whose name translates as "The totally Crazy Potato". It sounds horribly like a German version of Spud-U-Like, but it's really much better. Believe me, though the description I'm about to pass on to you may not improve that image. I hope that those of you who have used my guides "out in the field", will by now afford me a degree of trust (and if you don't, what on earth are you doing still reading my junk?). I was strangely seduced by this seemingly appalling epitome of all that is bad about the modern gastronomic world. I don't give it that high a rating but, hey, for this style of eatery, it's the equivalent of three Michelin stars.

Where I was immediately reminded of - for no particular reason - was the estate pub nearest to where I lived in West Swindon (the Swindon of the West). It's all the fake internal architectural bits, perhaps, such as a tiled roof over the bar. There is one room, though loads of twiddly bits of alcoves formed from demolition salvage break this up considerably. The "by the yard" old books on high shelves immediately brought into my mind another 1980's Swindon monstrosity of a pub: the one closest to my work. A combination of two design catastrophes - is the gestalt a masterpiece of kitsch? Don't ask me. I just drink the beer and check if the bar staff know their Aas from their Elblag.

Strangely, this mish-mash of historical débris is in a genuinely old building. But, in a sort of mirror of the interior, a modern block of flats is adjacent and actually extends above this house. Spooky, eh?

The beers include a very pleasant Mönchshof Premium Schwarzbier, the Weißbier products of the Kulmbacher brewery in bottle and draught Sternquell, which, sadly, is a poor shadow of its former magnificent self.
Rating: **   Public transport:

Paulaner-Restaurant Der Zwinger (in Hotel Kaiserhof)

Wartburgallee 2,
99817 Eisenach.
Tel. 03691 - 213513
Fax: 03691 - 203653
Email: info@kaiserhof-
eisenach.bestwestern.de
http://www.kaiserhof-
eisenach.bestwestern.de/

Opening   hours: Mon-Sun
11:00 - 24:00
Number of draught beers: 4
Number of bottled beers: 3
Regular draught beers:

Paulaner Urtyp 1634
Paulaner Premium Pils
Paulaner Dunkles
Paulaner Hefeweizen

Food: Snacks, meals.
You'll all be bored to death by me banging on about this yet again, but I do greatly admire Paulaner for their chain of tied houses. I may have growing doubts about certain of their beers (the dreaded hop-extract), but they do have some great boozers. When in a new town and desperate, my first move is to check for the presence of a Paulaner outlet.

You German experts may well have heard of Dresden's renowned Zwinger museum, part of that city's distinctive skyline. Now, it's only while I was browsing through a German kid's guide to castles (coincidentally in the bookshop on Eisenach's main shopping thoroughfare Karlstraße), that I realised what a Zwinger was. It means "bailey" - one of the outer walled courtyards of a castle. Whether the Zwinger in question here is a reference to Wartburg castle (at the top of the hill up which Wartburgallee winds) or Dresden is unclear.

Hotel Kaiserhof dominates a corner immediately in front of the only preserved tower of the city wall. The style of the building is typical for the period called in Germany "Gründerzeit", the age of rapid economic expansion preceding World War One. It's a form of architecture I've got quite a soft spot for. OK, we're heading into town from the station (another beautiful building from the same era) and the fork at Kaiserhof gives you two options: up the hill to the castle; through the gate into town. If you're on foot, going left is a bad option, unless your destination is the brewery (at the bottom of the hill, on the left) or the castle, a chest-bursting climb of a mile or two.

Where were we? I remember - I was trying to tell you about this Paulaner pub. It's in basement of the hotel, the main advantage of which is that it's completely separated from the hotel part of the structure. You can see the windows half sticking out from the pavement in my snap above. Now there's a funny story about the semi-subterranean nature of this boozer. I'm told that during periods when miniskirts were popular, seats close to the windows were most favoured by young gentlemen. Despite their low elevation, they found the outlook admirable.

At some point I will eventually tell the more patient amongst you what it's like inside. Well, not really any great surprises. There's a single L-shaped room in a typical Paulaner style. Dark-panelled walls, pine tables and chairs. Hopefully my photo isn't so dark that you can't get the idea without me using up any of my lyrical inspiration. Slightly odd are the waitresses who, true to Bavarian tradition, are clad in dirndls. Unlike Bavaria, none of them looked like they were drawing their pensions yet. Got the idea - it's almost like being in Munich (not, by any means, an unpleasant thought). They're making a good attempt to hide the panelling with old photos and newspaper clippings, but will need another year or two to complete the job.

One last point about the interior. Christophe, it defies the law of toilet symbols you told me. The male and female figures on the bog doors are indisputably fat, yet the toilets themselves are the epitome of modernity and cleanliness. I would go far as to say, the best quality toilets I found in the town.

The food is a combination of Thuringian and Bavarian, which suits me just fine. Any menu with a high dumpling quota scores highly with me. No arguments about either the quality or quantity (this is Germany, after all) of the nosh.

Beer - well it can't come as much of a shock that they have a load of Paulaner ones. I would steer away from their pale bottom-fermenting beers - the hop-extract taste screws them up a treat. The Dunkles and wheat beers fare much better, being lightly-hopped. Rating: **** Public transport:

Waldgasthof Sängerwiese

Sängerwiese 1,
99817 Eisenach.
Tel. 03691 - 20 32 72
Fax: 03691 - 20 32 72

Email: info@gasthof-saengerwiese.de
Homepage: www.gasthof-saengerwiese.de

Opening hours: Mon-Sun 10:00 - 18:00
Number of draught beers: 2
Number of bottled beers: 3
Regular draught beers:

Hasseröder Premium Pils
Eisenacher Schwarzer Drachen

Food: Snacks €2-8, meals €3-17, beer €2.40 a half litre.
I wouldn't pay too much attention to the address. What it really should say is, "half way up a hill, in a forest, just outside town". I had the good fortune:

a) to have a father-in-law who's a local taxi driver
b) to be walking with the assistance of a crutch (it's a very, very long story that I won't be sharing with you)

so I didn't have to walk up the hill like you will have to. Sorry, it's emergency vehicles only.

"How could you have got the full appreciation of the beautiful surroundings in the Thüringer Wald national park, without putting in the work?" I hear you ask. Well, getting an hour's peace away from the bloody kids, left me in a very appreciative mood, believe me.

You're no doubt getting impatient with these personal asides and would like a few more hard facts. Here we go then. Sängerwiese is a fairly small pub/restaurant, in the middle of a wood (as I have already explained), decorated in a folksy but simple manner. So you're got the trademark check tablecloths and the slightly less grandmotherly dead animal skulls hung above the wood panelling. There are too separate rooms in addition to the DDR-style taproom.

The menu is stuffed with traditional Thuringian dishes (you'll be feeling stuffed after many of them), including plenty of game. For those of you on a budget there is a special menu that would put a smile on the face of the meanest miser. The "Ostalgie Menu" contains a selection of meals once common in DDR pubs. What makes especially tempting is that not only are the meals are exactly the same as they were, so are the prices. You can get a full meal for under 3 euros! It's amazingly good value.

You would be surprised how many portraits of Honecker, which used to hang in every pub in the DDR, are still knocking around. (I have one myself, somewhere, but my wife keeps taking it down and hiding it.) Quite often, as in this case, their location isn't as respectful as in former times. But it's nice to think that Erich is still keeping an eye on us. It was amusing to observe the efforts to whip up some sort of personality cult over a bloke, let's face it, with less charisma than John Major's underpants.

Ostalgie I interpret as a healthy phenomenon. In the immediate days after reunification everyone tried to pretend the previous 40 years somehow hadn't taken place. People now feel safe to express fond memories of elements of the DDR period, without coming on as some sort of unrepentant SED hard-liner. More and more DDR-memorabilia forms an integral part of pub interior design. I don't know what West Germans make of it, but it certainly brings a nostalgic tear or two to my eyes.

Also a small hotel with 6 double rooms. In the warmer months, there is a beer garden. Rating: ***** Public transport:

V Now

Berlin

Berlin is still a special place for me. And not special in the school or needs way.

When I say Berlin, I mean East Berlin. A few moments last year in Kreuzberg aside, I've barely spent five minutes in West Berlin. Other than hanging around in railway stations.

I feel at home in East Berlin. No idea why. Perhaps just all the time I've spent there. And all the happy times. Very happy times. With the woman I love in an exotic and exciting city. That it edges out 1986 Prague as bestest place ever should tell you everything.

The Berlin International Beer Festival is always a good excuse to revisit the city. That it's held on the street with the best assemblage Stalinist architecture in the world is another encouragement. Friedrichshain. My new favourite bit of Berlin. Especially now I've found that Getränkemärkt with all the good Bavarian beer.

If I squint, I can still see the DDR. Weird feeling nostalgic for a totalitarian state. Though it's really the prices that get my wallet itching.

2016

Köpenick

Dolores and I really got to know each other in Berlin. We'd met a few times, corresponded a lot. Truth comes when you look into each other's eyes.

That we met in Berlin wasn't by whim or design. We couldn't easily meet anywhere else, Dolores being a citizen of East Germany.

In the cold dark days of the, er, Cold War, travelling to an Eastern block country was a right palaver. You had to go to the embassy to apply for a visa. A total pain. Berlin, though, was another story.

Weird rules applied in Berlin. Despite being the capital of the DDR, you didn't need a visa in advance like everywhere else in the country. You could buy one at the door. For 24 hours. Nae probs, a weekend is only 48 hours, just need to recross the border once.

Already living in Amsterdam. I could jump on a train Friday night and be in Berlin by 6 AM. Leave East Berlin and re-enter it without leaving Friedrichstrasse station and get another 24 hours. Then take the night tram back to the flat. Happy days.

We must have spent at least a dozen weekends in Berlin in 1987 and 1988. Plenty of time to explore the city. My visa was only valid in Berlin, but fortunately the city's boundaries are very generous. There was a large area I could legally visit. Though, in reality, I could probably have jumped on a train to Leipzig and no-one would have been the wiser.

I can't remember why we visited Köpenick. It might have been because of the palace. There's a baroque job that used to belong to the Prussian royal family. Frederick the Great used it. Or it may have been simply because that was as far as I could go and remain in Berlin.

Eating in the Ratskeller, I do remember. Under a grand gothic revival vaulted cellar. Quite posh, but, it being the DDR, still dirt cheap. For me. All those Ostmarks I was forced to buy had to get used up somehow. In particular, I remember what I drank. Because it was a first time thing. Tokay.

The Tokay I'd read about in Gide's "Les Faux Monnayeurs". It seemed wonderfully exotic. Not something I'd come across in the pubs of Leeds or Newark. Seeing it in the DDR was a surprise. It didn't disappoint. Feeling supremely sophisticated, I sipped it slowly.

"Do you fancy going to Köpenick, Dolores?"

"What's there?"

"Don't you remember eating there before we were married? In the Ratskeller."

"Yes. So?"

"Would you fancy going back? There's also a little brewery close by."

"Why is that no surprise?"

On the way to the S-Bahn station we drop by the Getränkemarkt. To look for Tannenzäpfle with the retro fifties label. I can't find any so pick up a bottle of Tegernsee Spezial instead. Not sure why. But a spare bottle of beer is always handy to have to hand.

It's a surprisingly quick journey, despite the distance and a change in Ostkreuz. But I'm still in urgent need of a wee when we arrive in Köpenick.

"I need a wee. I'm going to nip into that pub."

Dolores declines and heads instead for the chemist opposite.

It's not the fanciest of pubs. But the barmaid insists on pouring my Pils the slow, multi-step way. All very nice, except when you're waiting for her to finish so you can rush to the bog.

There's a new shopping centre next to the station. That wasn't there before. I remember it looking like typical late 19th-century Berlin. Except perhaps a little crumblier. Past the shopping centre, it's more like what I remember. Though obviously much less crumbly.

When we get to the Rathaus I ask Dolores "Fancy eating in the Ratskeller?"

"It looks posh. Probably too expensive."

I check the price list and it's remarkably reasonable. Cheap enough even for Dolores. In Amsterdam we'd be limited to eating in FEBO for a similar price.

Inside it looks . . . . well, you'll have to wait until next time to discover about Ratskeller's interior. Because it's time for my bed now.

Köpenick (part two)

It is with a certain amount of dread that I walk down the steps to the Keller. Have they have fucked it up?

Luckily, they haven't. Little has changed from my memories, other than a coat of paint and a new bar counter. Still looks pretty classy. Much classier than the prices.

There's a smattering of other diners, but not too many. It is after 2 PM, so not that surprising. We grab a table for two next a long and very nicely laid out one. Very posh.

It's been at least 10 minutes since my last beer. Best order something quickly. Oh look, they've got Köstritzer Schwarzbier on draught. Not had a pint of that for ages. That'll do nicely. Dolores opts for a Wernesgrüner Pils. I'm impressed by how DDR the beer selection is. They may well have sold Wernesgrüner in the old days, it being fairly posh here back then, too. Can't say I was ever that impressed with the stuff myself or Radeberger. I much preferred the Pilseners of Thüringen.

We're only after something light. Dolores opts for one of her favourite things: raw minced pork.

"Not much cooking for the chef to do there." I quip.

Did I mention that Dolores's paternal grandmother was from East Prussia? Dolores's paternal grandmother came from East Prussia. Which is why Dolores knows how to make Königsberger Klopse, a type of boiled meatball. After I order a portion, I realise I've a bit of a Kö- theme going on: Ratskeller Köpenick, Köstritzer Schwarzbier, Königsberger Klopse.

We're halfway through our meal when we realise why the long table looks so posh. A wedding party turns up. It's slightly odd when the speeches start, as we're sitting right next to them. Like less fashionable relations at a satellite table.

Did I mention how ridiculously cheap it is? A meal each, 2 pints for me and a pint and a half for Dolores comes to €32.80. A bargain. Especially as it was also really tasty.

All prandialled-up, we set off to stretch our legs a little. Our destination is Schloss Köpenick, a baroque palace. I have vague memories of visiting it last time we were down this way all those years ago. It's not much of a leg-stretcher, being not much more than 100 metres.

The palace itself doesn't seem to be open, so we go and sit in the garden. Just as well I've my emergency pint with me. I suck on that as we watch another wedding party have their photos taken. I can see why they chose here. It's a very pretty spot. And a short stroll from the Rathaus where I assume the official formalities took place.

It's pretty obvious this must have originally been a castle. The centre of Köpenick is on an island and the Schloss is on a smaller island off that. An obvious spot for a settlement and fortification.

When the photographer has done his work and my emergency pint is used up, it's time to move on. Not to worry. A brewery is just a few steps away. One I'd wanted to visit for a while.

Not just any old brewery. What claims to be the smallest commercial brewery in Germany. I won't argue with them. Their kettle is tiny. Really tiny. Most serious home brewers have larger kit.

It's a strange sort of place. Basically a glass cube in the middle of the square. There's a bit of seating inside, but far more room at outside tables. Which is where me and Dolores park our arses, trying to stay upwind of the smokers. Of which there are plenty.

For a German brewpub, the beer range isn't bad. Not just the dreaded Helles, Dunkles, Weizen trio, all served very green. I don't understand how anyone can drink the godawful Helles many brewpubs offer. Here there's also a Pale Ale a Kirsch-Chilli Bier and, what most impressed me, Köpenicker Moll, a local style.

They say on their website that the recipe was developed from archive material and in collaboration with a historian. But I've learnt to be pretty cynical about these things. Without more details about the recipe, it's hard for me to judge how authentic the beer is.

The beers are pleasant enough. Definitely drinkable, which isn't always a given. We have a couple before wending our way back to the S-Bahn station.

It's been a fun day out. Köpenick hasn't disappointed.

Ratskeller Köpenick,
Alt Köpenick 21,
12555 Berlin.
Tel: + 49 (0)30 6 55 51 78
Fax: +49 (0)30 65 47 27 49
E-Mail: verkauf@ratskeller-koepenick.de
http://www.ratskeller-koepenick.de

Draught beers: Wernesgrüner Pils, Köstritzer Schwarzbier, Erdinger Hefeweizen and Guinness

Schlossplatzbrauerei Köpenick
Grünstraße 24
12555 Berlin- Köpenick
Tel. : 030 42096876
m.rubbert@schlossplatzbrauerei-koepenick.com
http://www.schlossplatzbrauerei-koepenick.com/

Index